AN IDEAS INTO ACTION GUIDEBOOK

Building an Authentic Leadership Image

IDEAS INTO ACTION GUIDEBOOKS

Aimed at managers and executives who are concerned with their own and others' development, each guidebook in this series gives specific advice on how to complete a developmental task or solve a leadership problem.

LEAD CONTRIBUTORS	Corey Criswell
	David Campbell
CONTRIBUTORS	Vidula Bal, Al Calarco,
	Craig Chappelow, Sara King,
	Laura Quinn, Cresencio Torres,
	Ellen Van Velsor

DIRECTOR OF PUBLICATIONS	Martin Wilcox
EDITOR	Peter Scisco
ASSOCIATE EDITOR	Karen Lewis
WRITER	Rebecca Garau
DESIGN AND LAYOUT	Joanne Ferguson
CONTRIBUTING ARTISTS	Laura J. Gibson
	Chris Wilson, 29 & Company

CCL No. 436
ISBN No. 978-1-60491-003-2

CENTER FOR CREATIVE LEADERSHIP
POST OFFICE BOX 26300
GREENSBORO, NORTH CAROLINA 27438-6300
336-288-7210
WWW.CCL.ORG / PUBLICATIONS

AN IDEAS INTO ACTION GUIDEBOOK

Building an Authentic Leadership Image

Corey Criswell and David Campbell

Center for
Creative
Leadership

NORTH AMERICA EUROPE ASIA

www.ccl.org

The Ideas Into Action Guidebook Series

This series of guidebooks draws on the practical knowledge that the Center for Creative Leadership (CCL®) has generated, since its inception in 1970, through its research and educational activity conducted in partnership with hundreds of thousands of managers and executives. Much of this knowledge is shared—in a way that is distinct from the typical university department, professional association, or consultancy. CCL is not simply a collection of individual experts, although the individual credentials of its staff are impressive; rather it is a community, with its members holding certain principles in common and working together to understand and generate practical responses to today's leadership and organizational challenges.

The purpose of the series is to provide managers with specific advice on how to complete a developmental task or solve a leadership challenge. In doing that, the series carries out CCL's mission to advance the understanding, practice, and development of leadership for the benefit of society worldwide. We think you will find the Ideas Into Action Guidebooks an important addition to your leadership toolkit.

Table of Contents

EXECUTIVE BRIEF

Many leaders assume that image building is superficial and therefore unimportant, but you can benefit from knowing how you come across to others and making improvements if necessary. This doesn't mean creating a false image. The idea is to recognize genuine aspects of yourself that should be coming across to other people—but aren't. Crafting your image requires you to gain a clear picture of the image people are currently perceiving, decide what image you would like to portray, develop the skills to close the gap, and practice. It takes skill and practice to be comfortable in your leadership role and to have an image to match.

A Leader's Image

Your image is the concept that others form about you as a result of the impressions you make on them. Your effectiveness as a leader is tied to your image. Your ability to project a leadership presence in the eyes of employees, customers, other important constituencies, and the general public is closely related to your ability to do your job well. Your image, then, can be either an asset or a liability as you engage in the tasks and roles of leadership.

Many people make the mistake of assuming that paying attention to image building is superficial and therefore unimportant. However, leaders can benefit from knowing how they come across to others and making improvements if necessary. A study of 150 senior executives who attended CCL's Leadership at the Peak program shows that the image leaders convey has a significant correlation to perceptions of their leadership skill. In this study, leaders who conveyed a strong vision were rated higher on several important factors than those who conveyed a weaker vision—factors such as the ability to lead change, being dynamic, competence in strategic planning, being farsighted, inspiring commitment, being original, and having a strong executive image. Each of these factors is tied to specific behaviors and can therefore be improved through awareness and practice.

Image is commonly thought of as being based on various external aspects of a person, such as physical appearance or formal status. Your image is affected by these elements, but it is also affected by any impression you make on others. Your personality, behavior, body language, and speaking style all contribute to your image.

Did I Say That?

These are some typical behaviors and their common interpretations. Can you think of others?

Behaviors	Interpretations
lack of eye contact	deceptive
crossed arms	defensive
"...um...uh..."	nervous
shifting eyes	not trustworthy

Your image may be the conduit through which people initially know you; it can have a great impact on how they get to know you as a person and as a leader. Whether someone is getting to know you through a first meeting, over time, or even through the media, your image is being broadcast and your reputation is being formed. In the short term, image is important because you have only a few minutes to interact before others draw conclusions about you. In the long term, your image is tied to your credibility and effectiveness. In particular, people value consistency in what you say, what you do, and how you appear.

Fortunately, you can have a great deal of control over the image others have of you. Laura Morgan Roberts of Harvard Business School puts it this way: "People manage impressions through their nonverbal behavior (appearance, demeanor), verbal cues (vocal pitch, tone, and rate of speech, grammar and diction, disclosures), and demonstrative acts (citizenship, job performance)."

Crafting your image requires you first to gain a clear picture of the image people are currently perceiving, then to decide what image you would like to portray, and finally to develop the skills to close the gap.

Why Manage Image?

Why should leaders focus on understanding and managing their image? Here are several reasons:

- **You already have an image. The question is whether it's the image you want and need to have to be an effective leader.** People form opinions of others all the time. By being mindful of your current image and taking a proactive approach to improve where necessary, you can close the gap between the way others perceive you and your desired image. This is particularly important in today's large, geographically dispersed organizations where employees may spend little time with senior managers and, therefore, see them only in limited contexts.

- **People will make assumptions about you.** In the absence of solid information and frequent communication, people often make assumptions. And what they invent is likely to be a distortion of the truth. Your image as a leader runs the same risk. In the absence of credible information and personal insight about contacts with you, people may reach erroneous conclusions about who you are, what your values are, what kind of leader you are, and how well you are doing in your job.

- **Your image speaks louder than you do.** You may spend a lot of time creating and polishing what you have to say—preparing documents and presentations, crafting your message. But all that information is interpreted in the context of who you are—more precisely, who people *think* you are. *How* you say

---

When Do You Create Your Image?

A leader's image is constantly being created. Your ongoing behavior and attitude will confirm people's impressions of you—or refute them. Here are some opportunities that permit you to create and solidify your image as an effective leader. Each one offers opportunities to practice behaviors that will create an effective leadership image. Can you think of others?

- one-on-one meetings
- phone, videoconference, and e-mail discussions
- presentations to employees
- riding in the elevator
- board meetings
- media interviews
- interacting in the cafeteria or parking lot
- traveling with others on business
- events or locations outside work

---

something has a great impact on *what* people hear you say. Your message is carried strongly by intonation, body language, and demeanor. Your words, actions, and manner need to be congruent; otherwise you will be doubted. If you've just announced a major change to the organization, for example, employees are not likely to retain the details, but they will remember how you communicated the information and react to your attitude and disposition. Based on the impression you make, they may say things like "He doesn't believe a word of what he's saying" or "He's really excited about this new system."

Gain a clear picture of the image people are currently perceiving, decide what image you would like to portray, and develop the skills to close the gap.

---

* **People seek personal connections.** Image is interpreted through the lens of personal preference. Your image is often greatly influenced by your personal connections with others, or their being able to identify with you in some personal way. At CCL, the power of the personal is apparent in our leadership development programs. During the initial introductions, participants are asked to tell the class about their work, a current leadership challenge, and a fun fact about themselves, such as a

hobby, a travel experience, a family adventure, or a unique interest or skill. The other participants often forget the professional details, but they readily recall the personal information.

- **People have high expectations.** We want leaders to be likeable, personable, regular people; at the same time we want them to be above reproach, better than average, and demonstrative of our high standards. In the days of YouTube and MySpace,

Image and Authenticity

Many of the executives who attend CCL's Leadership at the Peak program struggle with their authenticity as leaders. They often feel such a strong need to maintain their executive image that it becomes the number one obstacle to their authenticity. They are unsure how to be authentic, genuine leaders and at the same time work to craft their image.

Our suggestion to individuals who are struggling with this quandary is to rethink their understanding of "executive image." Often, they have defined it more narrowly than they need to. They have unnecessarily put tight limits on themselves, trying to maintain a powerful façade, when revealing their personality and humanness is a better sign of effective leadership.

As you work to convey an effective leadership image, keep in mind that working on your image is not about faking anything. It's about surfacing and polishing behaviors and skills that allow your authentic self to be most effective.

camera and video phones, and instant communication, a leader's image can be tanked or tarnished with one misstep or incongruous action. Impressions can be hard to live down.

- **Long careers demand investment.** You invest in your career in many ways: education and training, experience, networking, and goal setting. Don't let a negative or poor image limit or sabotage your leadership potential. Just as you pay attention to developing the technical expertise and interpersonal skills needed to be successful in your job, you should develop your image in a way that serves you as a leader.

We want leaders to be likeable, personable, regular people; at the same time we want them to be above reproach, better than average, and demonstrative of our high standards.

- **Your image affects the performance of the people around you, especially your direct reports.** If you come across as a person who is productive, optimistic, thorough, and fair, these characteristics will be seen as desirable among your direct reports. The reverse is also true. Scheming and sloppiness can also be transmitted.

Leaders' Misperceptions of Image

Many leaders draw back from the idea of managing their image, thinking it is irrelevant or even dishonest or manipulative. Common misperceptions leaders have about image include the following:

✗ **Only celebrities and politicians manage their image.** It may be true that the very famous (or those who want to be) pay more attention to their image than most of us do. But consciously or unconsciously, we manage our image all the time. If you've ever practiced giving a speech, carefully considered your wardrobe, or labored over your resume, you've been working on your image.

✗ **People know me; what's there to manage?** People don't know what you don't show. You may have agonized over a difficult decision, but if your behavior doesn't reflect that process, others may see you as rash and uncaring.

✗ **What you see is what you get.** When you've established solid, long-term relationships, your mind-set may be fairly predictable to others. But in today's large organizations and global communication channels, you are likely to interact with many people only on a limited basis. A fifteen-minute interaction can define you in another's eyes for many years.

✗ **Creating an image is about being fake.** Some people choose to create an external image that is different from their true selves. Falsehood or hypocrisy often is revealed as scandal in the news or years later in biographies. But the creation of an effective leadership image is not about faking it or putting on a show. It's not about trying to project a false image. It's the opposite: projecting yourself fully as a leader in a way that's consistent with who you are and what you do. It's about coming across to people in a way that does you and your organization justice.

✗ **My position creates my image.** Your role contributes to your image, but does not define it. For instance, Kofi Annan, former Secretary-General of the United Nations and recipient of the 2001 Nobel Peace Prize, is often seen as more understated, humble, and introspective than one might expect for a person in that role.

The image leaders convey has a significant correlation to perceptions of their leadership skill.

Assessing Your Image

It isn't easy to see ourselves the way others see us. But a clear-eyed look at the image others have of you is essential for understanding to what extent your image is helping or hindering your effectiveness. Use the worksheet on page 17 to begin this process. Then continue with the questions and activities that follow.

Questions for Reflection

- What three words would you use to describe your leadership image? What words would your boss use? What words would your direct reports use? What about other constituencies?

- What feedback have you gotten about your image and how you communicate? What comments have you heard that may be clues to how others view you?

- What image is conveyed by leaders in your organization? How well does your image fit? Context matters. Something that contributes to a positive image in one organization may detract from it in another. For example, you may like to use storytelling as a way to generate buy-in, but your organization may operate with a "just the facts" mentality.

- Think of a time when your image worked to your advantage. How could you replicate that success more often? Think of a time when your image didn't serve you well. What could you do differently in the future?

- Consider various scenarios: one-on-one, prepared speeches, large groups, extemporaneous speeches, etc. In what situations

A First Look

Reflecting on the past couple of months, review each of the image-related behaviors listed below. On a scale of 1 to 4 (low to high), rate each item according to how skilled you think you are. In the next column, indicate how often you put that behavior to use, again using a scale of 1 to 4 (very rarely to very often). Finally, you might have other people rate you too. Ask a coworker, boss, or direct report to give you feedback.

How Well	How Often	Behavior
_____	_____	I pay attention to my image.
_____	_____	I consider the image I project in all communication channels: large presentations, one-on-one, e-mail, etc.
_____	_____	I consider the image I project to people at all levels: bosses, coworkers, direct reports.
_____	_____	I am well prepared and express myself clearly.
_____	_____	My speaking style is clear and easily heard and understood.
_____	_____	I am optimistic.
_____	_____	My body language shows that I am comfortable in my role.
_____	_____	I am considered friendly.

do you feel strong and comfortable? When do you feel weak and uncomfortable?

Activities for More Information

- Sit in the hot seat. One component of CCL's Leadership at the Peak program simulates a media interview on a business talk show. You can do the same thing using the communications or human resources department in your organization. Have the interviewer ask the guest—you—about your vision for your company, department, or project, as well as questions about problem areas and successes. Videotape the session and debrief how you did with a group of trusted colleagues or friends. What did your on-camera behavior tell you about your image? Consider nonverbal behavior, vocal cues, and message delivery in your assessment.

- Seek feedback. Talk to people in your organization to get a better handle on your image or reputation. With some people, the direct approach will work; with others it is wise to look for clues and ask indirectly. Find out if your organization uses 360-degree assessments.

- Find a focus. Pick one image issue and focus on it for just one week. What do you notice about yourself? What do you do that supports the positive image you want to have? What is limiting or undermining you? You might even want to enlist a co-worker to "spot" you during the week. Have him or her observe you and give you feedback at the end of the week on your issue or challenge.

Image Busters

As you assess your current image, be on the lookout for the following image busters: common mistakes executives make that have a negative effect on their leadership image.

✗ **Too much seriousness.** Leaders don't need to be serious to be taken seriously. A smile and some warmth are good things. Leaders who are overly reserved look wooden, stiff, and uncaring.

✗ **Weak speaking skills.** In a media-saturated world, people know a good speaker when they hear one. The standard is high, and a leader with a flat or monotone vocal style, inappropriate volume, or poor diction isn't tolerated.

✗ **Lack of clarity.** Leaders who speak in vague, disjointed, or rambling sentences confuse people. If the message is unclear and nonspecific, the listeners will tune out and assume you don't know what you're talking about.

✗ **Self-absorption.** Leaders who overuse *I, me,* and *my* are isolating themselves and not engaging their audience. Even if something is your idea, your vision, and your responsibility, keep in mind that your job as a leader is much bigger than yourself.

✗ **Lack of interest.** When you were in school, which teachers captured your attention and imagination? The energetic teachers who seemed to love their job? Or the ones who lectured dispassionately from the podium?

Energy, interest, and passion for their work are incomparable assets for leaders.

✗ **Obvious discomfort.** It's painful to watch a leader who is uncomfortable in front of a crowd or awkward in conversation. If you are tentative or uncomfortable in the roles you play, people begin to doubt your ability to be an effective leader—especially in difficult situations.

✗ **Others.** There's no shortage of ways to bust your image. Other possibilities include rambling, defensiveness, inconsistency, being out of shape, and lack of self-awareness.

Choosing Your Image

Developing your leadership image requires you to have a vision of that image. What image do you want to convey? What about you does not seem to come across in the best way? What kind of image is important for you to have in your organization or field?

In choosing your image and setting goals for improvement, you'll want to consider a range of possibilities. This is not to say, however, that you need to choose an image to put on and replace at whim. Managing your image is not about creating a false image; rather it is about recognizing genuine aspects of yourself that should be coming across to other people—but aren't for some reason. In fact, by considering the image that is expected in your line of work, you are also free *not* to develop your image in that direction. You will then be aware that your image may be working against you and decide to persevere . . . or to leave that situation.

To think about your desired leadership image, complete the activities in the worksheet on pages 22–23.

Closing the Gap

Developing your leadership image doesn't need to be an incredibly complicated process. Often, gaining the awareness of your current image and its limits goes a long way. If you realize you talk too fast when delivering bad news and are often viewed as nervous, for example, then you can make a conscious effort to take a breath, slow down, and remain calm.

To achieve your desired leadership image, you'll want to use techniques to help you address content, as well as verbal and nonverbal behaviors, including the following:

- **Tell stories.** Leaders who readily give interesting examples through their stories are engaging and more interesting. They respond to and influence the organizational culture when they tell stories about what happened, how a problem was solved, or someone who did something notable.

- **Master your message.** Clarity of thought and message is key. Think about what you want to say. Every question and conversation is an opportunity to share key ideas, vision, and values.

What Would You Like?

Choose your image. What would you like your image to show? Possibilities include humorous, considerate, empowering, credible, organized, productive, calm, flexible, well informed, etc. What behaviors—body language, vocal style, and message—would lead others to see you in this way? (Example: I would like for my team to see that I am credible. I need to work on my eye contact, body language, and tone of voice when I am talking about complex and difficult issues.)

_____

_____

_____

Watch and learn. Think about someone you've worked for or known who has an effective leadership image. List words that describe his or her image. Next, consider specific ways that the person behaves that enhance his or her image. (Example: "She was seen as trustworthy. She communicated to us often during a really difficult time. She kept us updated on the situation, but also told us when she didn't have the information or answers.) How could you adapt the person's behavior or do something similar to create an effective leadership image? Conversely, what might you learn from someone who has an ineffective leadership image?

_____

_____

_____

Plan ahead. Look at the image of people who have the job you'd like to have in two years. What is required of people in those roles in terms of image? Perhaps they need to be seen as well connected, comfortable being in the spotlight, skilled at giving media interviews or speeches, or able to engage with diverse groups of people. What could you do differently to show others that you are up for the task?

_____

_____

_____

Get visual. Find an image of your image! Is there a person whose image you admire? Find a photo of him or her and post it as a reminder. Are there other pictures or images that reflect your desired image? A rock climber to show your willingness to take on a challenge? A painting that symbolizes the feelings you hope to convey to employees? A place that speaks of the future? Whatever symbol or picture speaks to you, keep it as a reminder and for inspiration. List your ideas below; later you can look for pictures online or in magazines (or draw your own).

_____

_____

_____

_____

Strike a balance between too much detail and not enough; be sure you can talk about vision and concepts and show your grasp of the tactical.

- **Use vocal variety.** People listen better to a pleasant and appropriate speech pattern. Pay attention to your intonation, speed, diction, pacing, and volume. Do you regularly say "ummmm" or overuse a word? Do you forget to breathe and rush through what you have to say?

- **Focus on "we."** Leaders who use inclusive language ("we" and "us") inspire and draw on shared effort and interests.

- **Set a challenge.** Leaders need to show that they understand the context—including challenges. Use those challenges to motivate others and show confidence in the outcome. Be optimistic.

- **Show confidence.** Effective leaders use body language that shows they are relaxed and comfortable in their role. Even when leaders are in a tough situation or bearing bad news, they need to demonstrate that they are prepared to deal with it.

- **Smile.** You'll appear friendly if you tap into your personal warmth; one of the best ways to convey warmth is to smile. Often leaders don't relax or crack a smile unless they are talking about something personal: their child's school event, coaching a sports team, a recent vacation. Leaders with a friendly image know they are more effective, engaging, and interesting if they take the same tone when they talk about the business.

- **Consider visual impact.** They'll see you before they hear you, and nonverbal communication is powerful. Change your haircut or update your wardrobe. If you feel good about your appearance, you'll project an image of greater confidence.

Managing your image is not about creating a false image; rather it is about recognizing genuine aspects of yourself that should be coming across to other people—but aren't for some reason.

You might also draw on the expertise of others to jump-start a change and give you practice. Here are some ideas to consider:

- **Get a voice or speaking coach.** If your intonation or vocal style isn't creating a compelling image, work with someone trained to develop speaking skills.

- **Invest in media or presentations skills training.** Let the experts give you the tips you need if this is a weak area for you.

- **Take an acting class.** Learn to use your expression and voice to convey feeling.

- **Find a leadership coach.** He or she can help you address the issues you find especially challenging.

- **Practice your ability to respond to the unexpected.** Give improvisational theater a try.

- **Seek out a mentor.** Someone in your organization can give you feedback and ideas about how you can improve your leadership image.

- **Join Toastmasters.** Improve your public speaking skills by getting involved with this respected international organization.

- **Work with a speechwriter.** Get help crafting the tone and structure of your message. The practice you get by preparing for a formal speech or presentation will also improve your delivery in informal settings.

Consider your own image issues—areas in which there's a gap between the image you actually project and the image you want to project. Think through possible ways to close that gap. Use the worksheet on page 27 to record your thoughts and set your goals.

Practicing Your Image

Even Winston Churchill apparently had to practice and work on his image. The story goes that Churchill's valet overheard him talking while taking a bath and was concerned. The valet knocked and said, "Sir, to whom are you speaking? Is everything all right?" Churchill replied, "I am addressing the House of Commons!"

Setting Your Goals

List the image issues you want to work on. Next, list ways you can learn and practice. Finally, prioritize your list and set specific goals and timetables to accomplish them. An example is provided.

Image Issue	Ways to Improve	Goals and Timetable
I want to become a more engaging public speaker.	• Use storytelling as a technique. • Pay attention to how other speakers incorporate stories in their talks. • Read something about how to use stories. • Be on the lookout for events that are worth sharing.	At our next monthly division meeting, I'll use one or two stories, not just data, to help convey our group's performance. I'll ask Jack to give me feedback on my talk.

Practice may not make you perfect, but it will almost certainly help you make progress. Once you have taken a close look at your current image, chosen your desired image, and set goals for closing the gap, the best strategy for crafting your image is to practice. An effective leadership image that seems innate very likely is not. Many leaders work hard to get to the point that it looks easy. It takes skill and practice to be comfortable in your leadership role and to have an image to match.

Practice may not make you perfect, but it will almost certainly help you make progress.

Suggested Readings

Bunker, K. A., & Wakefield, M. (2005). *Leading with authenticity in times of transition.* Greensboro, NC: Center for Creative Leadership.

Cartwright, T., & Baldwin, D. (2006). *Communicating your vision.* Greensboro, NC: Center for Creative Leadership.

Hughes, R. L., & Beatty, K. C. (2005). *Becoming a strategic leader: Your role in your organization's enduring success.* San Francisco: Jossey-Bass.

Kirkland, K., & Manoogian, S. (1998). *Ongoing feedback: How to get it, how to use it.* Greensboro, NC: Center for Creative Leadership.

Klann, G. (2007). *Building character: Strengthening the heart of good leadership.* San Francisco: Jossey-Bass.

Stark, M. (2005, June 20). Creating a positive professional image. *HBS Working Knowledge.* Retrieved from http://hbswk.hbs.edu/archive/4860.html

Background

For many years the Center has worked with senior-level executives to hone their leadership skills through its Leadership at the Peak program. One component of the program is a videotaped, media-style interview. CCL uses the seven-minute interviews as a way to help executives understand the image they convey. These interviews have also been the basis for research that has shown the connection between a leader's image and leadership effectiveness.

During the interview, executives are asked to talk about their visions for their organizations, several business issues, an organizational success, and perhaps a failure—and finally, to answer a question about their lives outside work. While the TV interview is the form we chose, the principles of good image management are the same for any setting.

In addition to providing valuable information for the individual leader, the interviews have shown examples of what works and what doesn't when creating an effective leadership image. CCL and Philip T. Willburn, an organizational development and knowledge management consultant at SAIC, conducted a detailed analysis of the vision content and articulation of 150 LAP participant interviews.

CCL analyzed 150 executive responses to a question about vision. We measured their comments in terms of both content (what's included in the vision statement) and articulation (how executives delivered the message). Those metrics were then compared to executives' leadership skills as measured by two 360-degree assessments.

What we found was that the image leaders conveyed in delivering their messages had a significant correlation to perceptions of their leadership skill. Leaders who conveyed a strong vision were rated higher on several important factors than those who conveyed a weaker vision—factors such as the ability to lead change, being dynamic, competence in strategic planning, being farsighted, inspiring commitment, being original, and having a strong executive image.

Key Point Summary

Your image is the concept that others form about you as a result of the impressions you make on them. It can be either an asset or a liability as you engage in the tasks and roles of leadership.

Many leaders assume that image building is superficial and therefore unimportant. However, you can benefit from knowing how you come across to others and making improvements if necessary. Crafting your image requires you to gain a clear picture of the image people are currently perceiving, decide what image you would like to portray, and develop the skills to close the gap.

It isn't easy to see yourself the way others see you. But a clear-eyed look at the image others have of you is essential for understanding how your image is helping or hindering your effectiveness.

Developing your leadership image requires you to have a vision of that image. This doesn't mean choosing an image to put on and replace at whim. Managing your image is not about creating a false image; rather it is about recognizing genuine aspects of yourself that should be coming across to other people—but aren't for some reason.

This process doesn't need to be incredibly complicated. Often, gaining the awareness of your current image and its limits goes a long way. To achieve your desired leadership image, use techniques to address content, as well as verbal and nonverbal behaviors. You might also draw on the expertise of others. Once you have taken a close look at your current image, chosen your desired image, and set goals for closing the gap, the best strategy for crafting your image is to practice. It takes skill and practice to be comfortable in your leadership role and to have an image to match.

Ordering Information

TO GET MORE INFORMATION, TO ORDER OTHER IDEAS INTO ACTION GUIDEBOOKS, OR TO FIND OUT ABOUT BULK-ORDER DISCOUNTS, PLEASE CONTACT US BY PHONE AT 336-545-2810 OR VISIT OUR ONLINE BOOKSTORE AT WWW.CCL.ORG/GUIDEBOOKS.